EXPERIMENTS with MOTION

Contents

Movement

All things on earth move. Living things move by themselves, while non-living things need a push or a pull to get into motion.

A moving experience

How many different kinds of movements can you identity? Make a list.

The pictures below show some movements. Can you name them?

Did you know?

A flea can jump 200 times its own height.
There is a bamboo plant in Asia that can gain as much height in a day as you would in the first 10 years of your life.

Swift and slow

All things do not move at the same pace. Some movements are so slow that you hardly notice them, while others happen in a flash.

To measure how fast or how slow a thing moves, we refer to its speed. Speed is the distance something travels in a fixed time. A car moving at the speed of 60 kilometres per hour takes one hour to cover that distance.

Some examples of speed

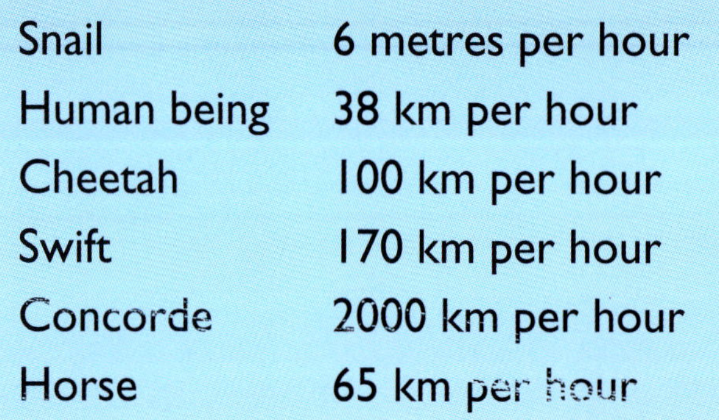

Snail	6 metres per hour
Human being	38 km per hour
Cheetah	100 km per hour
Swift	170 km per hour
Concorde	2000 km per hour
Horse	65 km per hour

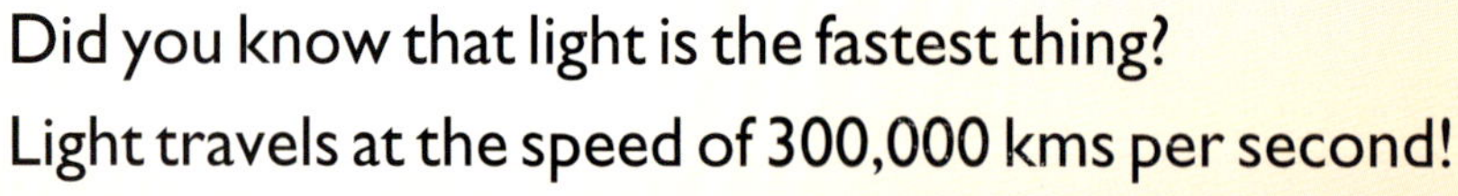

Did you know that light is the fastest thing?

Light travels at the speed of 300,000 kms per second!

Try this

From the world timings for men's 100 metres, 200 metres, 800 metres, 1500 metres and 5 kms, calculate the speeds of the athletes during their record runs. Can you justify the differences in the speeds?

How fast are you?

Measure your running speed.

You will need:

- a measuring tape
- a piece of chalk
- a watch
- a friend

1. Measure a distance of 50 metres with the tape.
2. Mark the two ends with chalk.
3. Run the distance while your friend notes the time taken.
4. Divide the 50 metres by the time noted by your friend. This gives your running speed in metres per second.

Time your journey

Next time you travel by car, note the time as well as the milometer reading at the beginning and at the end of the journey. Divide the change in the milometer reading by the time of travel, to get the average speed of your journey. Also, note the speedometer reading. Sometimes it may read 80 kmph and at other times, 40 kmph. It may even read 0 kmph if you are held up in a traffic jam. This is because the speed of a car is always changing.

The speedometer gives the speed of the car at any point of time, while the speed of the car over the journey gives you the average speed.

Rest and Motion

We know that things do not start moving by themselves. They seem to enjoy being at rest. This tendency of objects to stay where they are, is called the inertia of rest. Let's see how various objects display their inertia.

A stubborn coin

You will need:

- a glass
- a postcard
- a coin

1. Place the postcard on top of the glass.
2. Put the coin in the centre of the card.
3. Now flick the card away with a quick hit.

What happens to the coin? The stubborn coin refuses to leave its position of rest and drops into the glass.

The stick-on pile

1. Pile 4 carom coins, one on top of the other, at the centre of a carom board.
2. Place the striker on the baseline and strike the lowest coin in the pile. If hit properly, the coin will fly out leaving the rest of the pile undisturbed. The coins stay in place due to inertia.

Inertia depends on mass

You will need:

- a dictionary
- a book

1. Place the two books side by side on a table.
2. Push the books, first lightly, and then with increasing pressure. Which one moves first? Why?

Liquids also display inertia

1. Place a cup of water on a table.
2. When the water is still, suddenly pull the cup.
3. What happens? Some water will spill back due to its tendency to stay at the same place.
4. Now slide the cup of water on the table.
5. Then, suddenly stop the sliding cup. What happens? This time, some water will splash out in the direction in which the cup was sliding.

Did you know?

The water splashed forward due to its tendency to keep on moving. In fact, just as things at rest try to remain at rest, moving things try to maintain their motion. This is called the *inertia of motion*.

A bicycle ride

1. While riding a bicycle, suddenly apply the brakes.
2. You will notice that your body tends to move forward. Take care not to topple over.

You can also observe this while travelling in a bus or a car. When the car starts, your body leans backward, while it bends forward when the car stops.

Inertia of motion depends upon mass

You will need:

- a marble
- a cricket ball
- a sandpit

Drop the marble and the ball from the same height into the sandpit.

Which one sinks deeper? Why?

The cricket ball, being heavier, will have more inertia of motion than the marble, and so will go deeper into the sand.

Think it over

If all moving things have a tendency to keep moving, what stops them?

Force

A pull or a push is necessary to start or stop a movement. Such a pull or a push is called force. A force, however, does not always start or stop a moving object. A force also speeds up or slows down a moving body, thereby changing its motion.

A force fights against the inertia of a body

More force is required to change the motion of heavier objects. Check this.

You will need:

- a tea-trolley or a wheelbarrow
- some heavy books or stone

1. Push the wheelbarrow gently. It will roll easily. Stop it with one hand. You will feel a gentle reaction.
2. Load it with the stone. Try to push it. Does it move as easily as before? Why not?
3. Apply force till you overcome the inertia of the wheelbarrow and it starts rolling.
4. Stop the motion again with one hand. How does your hand feel this time?
   Try this with different loads.

A clothes peg shooter

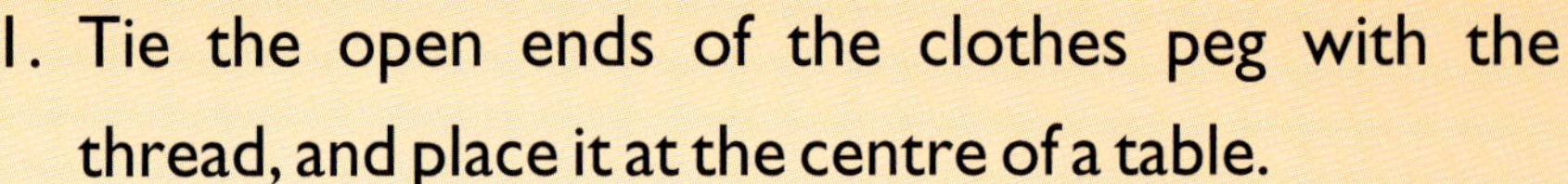

You will need:

- a clothes peg
- two short pencils of the same proportion
- two long pencils of the same proportion
- thread
- a matchbox

1. Tie the open ends of the clothes peg with the thread, and place it at the centre of a table.
2. Put the short pencils on either side of the clothes peg, close to the tied ends.
3. Carefully burn the thread. The pencils will shoot out in opposite directions.
4. Using one short and one long pencil and then two long pencils, repeat the above steps.

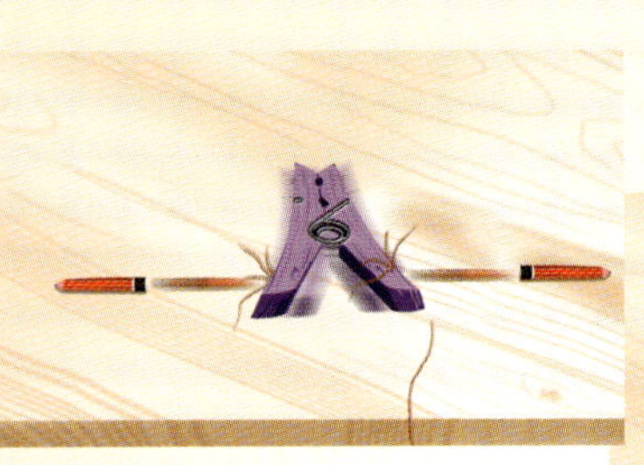

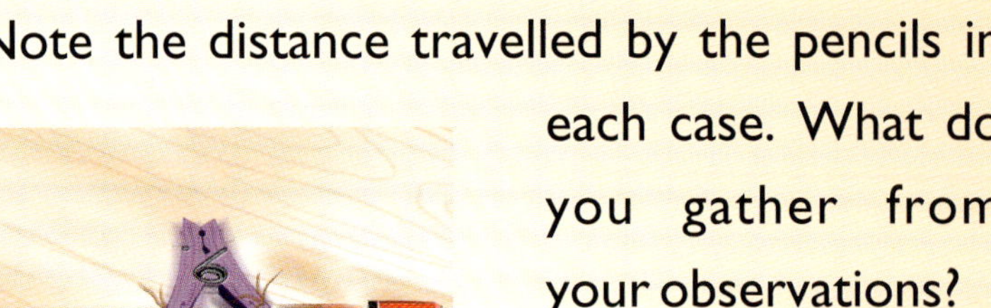

Note the distance travelled by the pencils in each case. What do you gather from your observations?

The direction of the force is important

Find out why.

1. Roll a tea-trolley.
2. Push it, once in the direction it is rolling in and then pull it with the same force in the opposite direction. How do the two forces affect the rolling motion?

A force applied in the direction of the motion increases its speed. The increase in the speed of a body in a fixed time is called *acceleration*. The greater the force applied, the higher is the acceleration produced.

The opposite of acceleration is *deceleration*. It is the rate of slowing down of a moving body. To slow down a body, a force has to be applied in a direction opposite to the direction of motion.

Newton's law of motion

Sir Isaac Newton, one of the greatest scientists of all times, gave a comprehensive explanation of force, motion and inertia. In the law of motion, Newton showed that whenever a force acts on an object, there is always an equal reaction that opposes the original force.

For example, if you push a wall with your hand, your hand will experience resistance. This is the force with which the wall pushes you back. It is equal to your push, but acts in the opposite direction.

To start moving, you need something solid to push against. When you move, you push the ground with your feet. The ground in turn gives you a forward push which sets you in motion.

A better start

You will need:

- a paper clip and a pair of pliers
- sellotape, two pencils and a rubber band

1. Straighten the paper clip and cut it in half.
2. Bend one end of each piece of wire with the pliers, as shown.
3. Tape the pieces of wire to the ends of the pencils so that the hooked ends project out. Loop the rubber band around the hooks and hold the pencils together.
4. Release your finger. The pencils will spring apart.
5. Now hold the pencils as before, and release only one pencil.

   How far does the single pencil spring? What helps it jump so much?

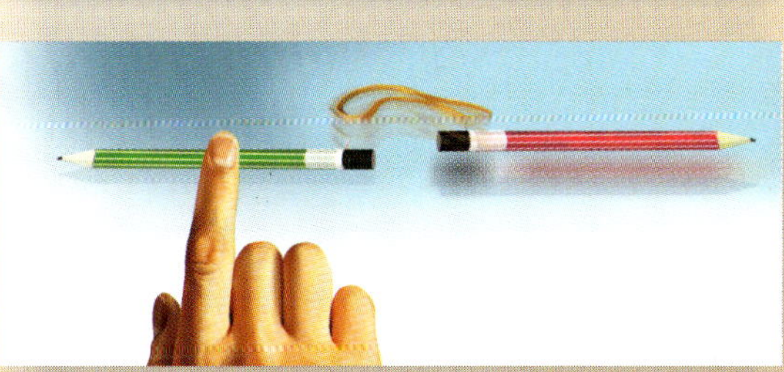

Everyday Forces

What stops a rolling football?

When a football rolls on the ground, the ground applies a force to stop its motion. This is called the *force of friction.* A frictional force appears whenever two surfaces come in contact. It is less in the case of smooth surfaces and more with rough ones.

1. Roll a marble on the floor. Put a mark where it stops. Measure the distance travelled by the marble.
2. Repeat step one on a newspaper, a sandaper, a gravelled path, a wet surface and on an oily surface. Compare the measured distances.
   What can you conclude from your results?

Sliding friction

You will need:

- a toy car
- two rubber bands
- a sloping surface

1. Choose a slope along which the toy car can slide down.
2. Lock the wheels of the car by criss-crossing the rubber bands over them on both sides.
3. Place the car on the slope.
   Does it slide down? Why not?

What makes things fall?

A stone does not move sideways without being pushed. It does not move upwards unless thrown or pulled up. But if you lift a stone and let it go, it will always fall towards the ground. This is due to the *force of gravity*. It is a force with which everything is pulled towards the earth. The acceleration is due to the gravitational force and is equal to 32 feet per second or 9.8 metres per second.

Which object reaches first?

You will need:

- a big stone
- a small stone
- a friend

1. Drop the two stones from the same height.
2. Ask your friend to note which one reaches the ground first.
   Are you surprised at the result? Though it seems that the heavier stone will reach first because more force acts on it, you should remember that its inertia is also more. All objects fall at the same rate.

The lazy paper

1. Drop a small piece of paper and a coin from the same height. Do they reach the ground at the same time?
   If all objects fall at the same rate, what holds up the paper? Air resistance does.
2. Will the result be the same if the experiment was carried out in vacuum?
3. Put the paper on the coin and drop the two. What happens this time? Can you explain why?

Curving through the air

If you throw a ball straight up, it falls down vertically. What happens when you throw it at an angle? When you throw a ball at an angle, it first goes up into the air because of the force with which you throw it. Then it starts to curve downwards due to the pull of gravity. The path travelled by the ball is called its *trajectory*.

Trace the trajectory

You will need:

- a drawing board
- a sheet of paper
- board clips
- a nail
- a rubber band
- a marble
- poster paint
- a spoon

1. Clip the paper on the board. Place the board at an angle.
2. Fix a nail to the bottom right of the board. Pass the rubber band through the nail.
3. Put a blob of paint in the spoon and roll the marble in it.
4. Pull back the rubber band and rest the marble on it. Release the band.

   The painted marble will trace out its trajectory on the paper. Change the angle of release and the starting velocity of the marble by varying the pull on the rubber band. How does this affect the height and the horizontal range of the trajectory?

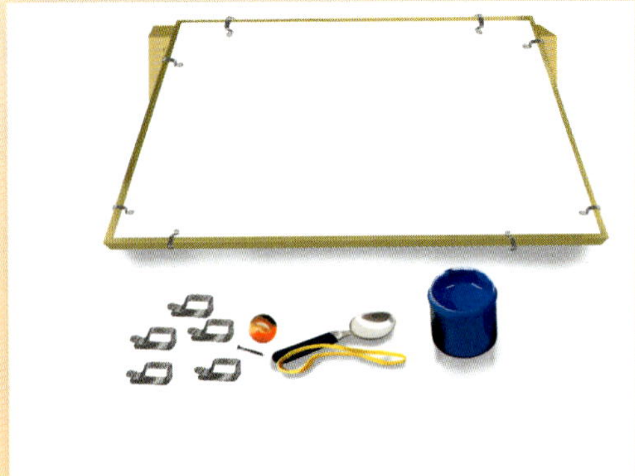

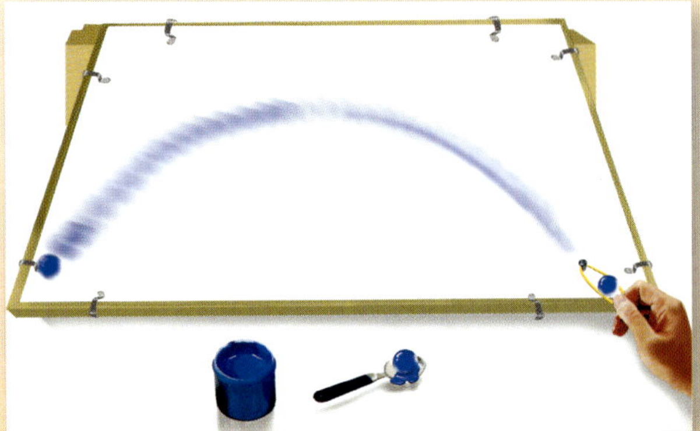

Centrifugal force

To know what this force is, let us perform this experiment.

You will need:

- a strong rubber band
- a stone

1. Tie the stone to the rubber band.
2. Whirl the stone around in a circle at arm's length. Can you see the stretch in the rubber? This is caused by a force acting on the stone directly outwards from the centre of the circle. It is called the *centrifugal force*. Centrifugal forces come into play whenever an object is moving in a circle.
3. Whirl the stone faster. The stretch on the rubber will increase because the centrifugal force increases with the speed of rotation.
4. While rotating, suddenly let go of the band. In which direction does the stone fly off?

   A centrifugal force occurs because a rotating object wants to keep moving in a straight line but is pulled around in a circle. This is why the stone speeds off in a straight line as soon as it is released.

The climbing marble

You will need:

- a marble
- a glass bowl

1. Put the marble in the bowl.
2. Whirl the bowl fast. What does the marble do?
   The marble wants to go off in a straight line, but is held back by the sides of the bowl. So it climbs up the sides!

A whirl wheel

You will need:

- a potter's wheel
- some small plastic toys

1. Arrange the toys around the centre of the wheel.
2. Turn it slowly. What happens to the toys? Increase the speed and watch the toys moving away from the centre. What do you think is pushing them?

A top designer

You will need:

- a hard cardboard
- a compass
- a used matchstick
- a pair of scissors
- some poster colours
- a paintbrush

1. Using the compass, draw a circle of 1.5" diameter on the cardboard.
2. Cut out the circle and pierce a small hole in the centre of the card.
3. Sharpen one end of the matchstick. Push it through the card. This is your top.

To colour the top, put small blobs of liquid colour near the centre. Then spin the top. Watch how the colour spreads. Make different coloured streaks using different colours.
Why do you think this happens?

A water trap

You will need:

- a small plastic bucket
- a 2' long piece of string
- a pair of scissors
- some water

1. Tie the string to the centre of the handle.
2. Fill half the bucket with water.
3. Swing the bucket over your head in a full circle. If you do it fast enough, the water will remain trapped inside the bucket even when it is upside down. This is due to the centrifugal force which pushes the water in an outward direction, away from the centre.

Another force

Did you feel a pull in your arm when you were swinging the bucket of water? This is the *centripetal force*. It is equal to the centrifugal force, but acts in the opposite direction. These two forces always occur together.

The solar system

The centrifugal force balances the force of gravity in the Solar System. In this case, the gravitational force acts as the centripetal force.

Action and reaction – Forces work in pairs.

A jet-propelled speedboat

You will need:

- a small tin with a tight lid
- a piece of thick cardboard
- a plastic carry bag
- glue
- a pair of scissors
- a large tub
- water
- a nail and a hammer
- some stiff wire

1. Cut the cardboard in the shape shown.
2. Cut and paste the plastic so as to wrap the cardboard boat.
3. Make a small hole at one end of the tin with the nail and the hammer.
4. Bend the wire to make a cradle for the tin. Fix it to the boat as shown.
5. Fill half the tin with water and fit the lid tightly.
6. Place the candle below the tin. Light it.
7. Now put the boat carefully in the tub of water.
8. As the water in the tin boils, steam will escape with force from the small hole. This will make the boat shoot forward with an equal and opposite force.

This principle of jet propulsion is used in rockets and jet engines.

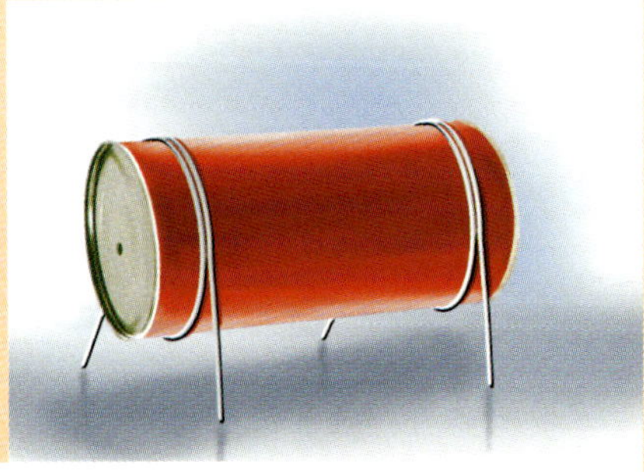

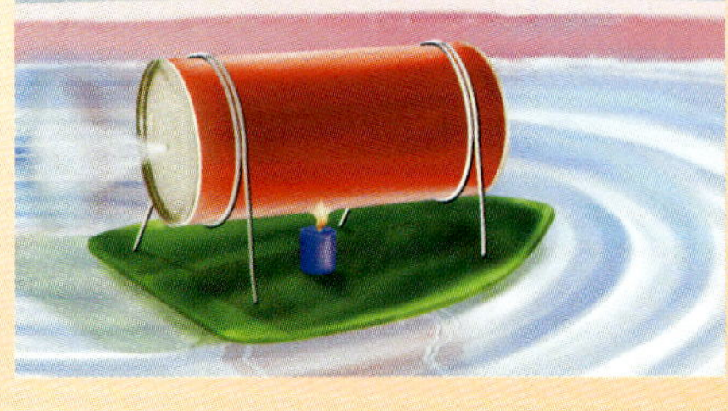

Some Common Movements

Walking

1. Walk on different surfaces like a hard floor, a carpet, a smooth floor, soft mud, sand and gravel. Which of these is the easiest to walk on? Why?
2. Close your eyes and walk on these surfaces. Can you feel the difference in the surfaces? What makes you aware that they are different?

When you walk, you always have at least one foot on the ground. As you push the ground with your foot, the ground pushes you forward. This is how you take a step forward.

A roller walker

1. Put a roller skate on.
2. Try to take a step forward. What happens? Since the rollers are smooth, the skate moves backward.

Stepping out of a boat

1. Step from a boat onto land. Make sure that the boat is loosely tied or held by someone.
   The boat slides in the water due to your push.
2. What do you think will happen if the boat is on the shore?

A jumping frog

You will need:

- a piece of hard cardboard
- a pencil
- a hairpin
- a rubber band
- sellotape
- a pair of scissors

1. Draw this frog shape on the cardboard.
2. Cut it out. Make a slot in the belly.
3. Loop the rubber band around the frog's belly.
4. Twist the loop twice with the hairpin, or till tight.
5. Cut out a very small piece of sellotape. Stick one part underneath the frog's hind legs. Stick the hairpin to the other part of the tape.
6. The band will try to untwist and pull the hairpin. This will make the frog jump.
   Can you say why?

Why doesn't a caterpillar run?

A caterpillar has 100 legs. It moves its legs in a wave so that they don't get entangled. This makes its walk slow — there's no question of it running.

Jumping

Our arms and legs have thick cords called *tendons* that join the muscles to the bones. We jump with the help of tendons.

Did you know?

Kangaroos can jump a distance of over 12 metres, at a height of 3 metres!

Turning

1. Draw two 50-metre tracks, one straight and the other circular.
2. Run along the tracks. Ask a friend to note the time. Are the two times different? Why?

While turning, all things experience a force that tries to make them go forward in a straight line. The sharper the turn, the higher the velocity, the more is this force. To balance this force, our bodies lean when we turn around a corner.

Observe this phenomenon next time you turn around on your bicycle. Recall what you learnt about centrifugal and centripetal forces in the last unit.
Roads are banked at the outer curve of a bend to help cars turn at high speeds.

Spinning

Spinning objects rotate around a fixed direction or axis and tend to resist any change in this direction.

1. Lift the front wheel of your bicycle off the ground.
2. Spin the wheel around and try to move the handlebars from side to side. Do you feel any force trying to stop you?

The speed of spinning depends on how the mass of the spinning body is distributed.

Make an air glider

You will need:

- a piece of cardboard
- a pencil
- a pair of scissors
- some modelling clay

1. Fold the card in half. Draw half a glider plane on one folded side.
2. Keep the card folded and cut along the lines. Open out the card and you will get your glider.
3. Put a little modelling clay on the nose of the glider.
4. If you push it gently, it will glide in the air. Air resistance will help your glider keep afloat in the air.
5. Note the symmetrical shape of the glider. Try making gliders with asymmetrical shapes. How well do they fly?

Try loading one wing of your glider. What happens?

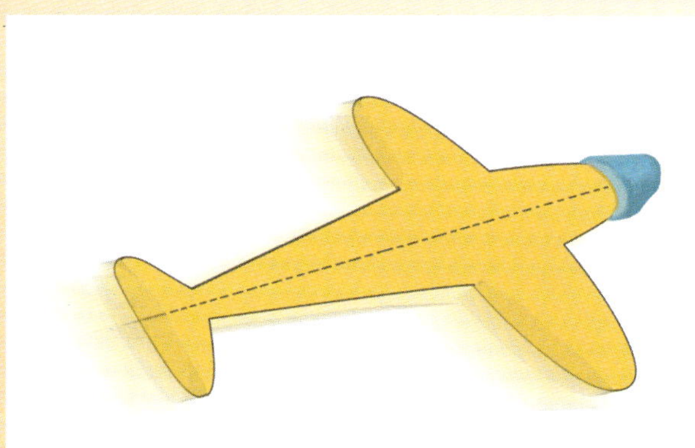

Flying

1. Hold a long piece of paper between your fingers so that the free end curls down.
2. Blow over the curved surface of the paper.

The rushing air will lift up the paper. This is called *airlift.* All flying things need to be airlifted. When an aeroplane runs on the runway, the air rushing over its wings gives it a lift.

Birds flap their wings to make the air flow over their wings and get the airlift.

Shape of wings

Observe the flight of different birds. You will find that some birds flap their wings more often than others. Some can go very high up in the sky.

Note the differences in their body shapes and weights and how they use these to their advantage while flying. Watch the movement of a bird while it takes off and lands.

Why do things float?

If you drop a stone and a cork in a tub of water, the stone sinks and the cork floats. Things float when the upward push of a liquid or a gas, called upthrust, is equal to the weight of the floating body.

Balloons float in air if they are filled with a gas called helium, because helium is lighter than air.

The art of swimming

Have you ever watched a fish swim?

1. Stand in front of an aquarium.
2. Note down the names, shapes and sizes of the various fish in the aquarium.
3. Observe how a fish uses its fins and tail to swim, dive and turn around. Fish use their side fins to guide them when they turn, dive or rise.

A deep-sea diver's flippers work like fins.

How do ducks swim?

Ducks have webbed feet that act very much like fins. They push the water with their feet and move forward.

Did you know?

A duck has oily feathers that help it remain afloat.

Simple Machines

A machine is any device that overcomes a force at one point by letting you apply a force at some other convenient point. It helps you to do work more easily. A knife and a pair of tongs are examples of very simple machines that you use every day. They are machines because in both you apply a force.

Lever

The knife and the tongs are examples of third-class levers where the effort is applied between the load and the fulcrum.

The wheelbarrow and the bottle opener are examples of second-class levers, where the load is between the effort and the fulcrum.

The see-saw is an example of a first-class lever in which the fulcrum lies between the load and the effort.

An easy lift

You will need:

- a fat book and a ruler
- a small wooden block

1. Arrange the items as shown in the figure.
2. Press the free end of the scale with your finger. Can you lift the book off thc ground?
3. Change the height of the wooden block, the position of the block, and the length of the ruler, and find out how it affects your lifting machine. What kind of a lever is it?

The inclined plane

You must have noticed that it is easier to pull something up a slope than to lift it. A slope is a simple machine.

Wheels

Today wheels are taken for granted. It is difficult to think of a time when the wheel had not been invented. But what exactly does a wheel do? It lessens the friction offered by the ground, thereby making movement easier and smoother.

A simple experiment will show you how this happens.

You will need:

- a fat book
- 4 round pencils
- a clipboard
- a rubber band

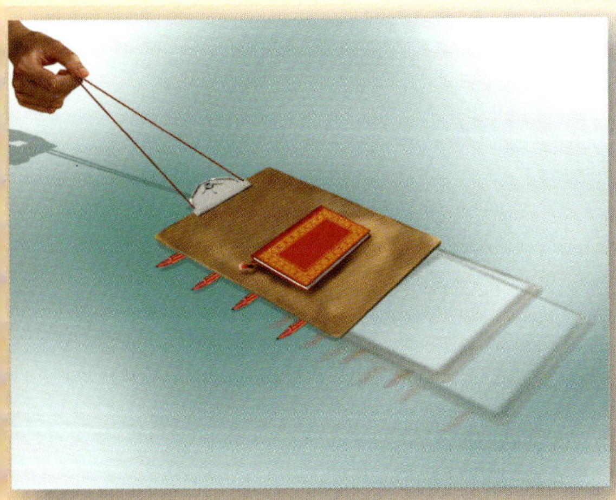

1. Put the book on the clipboard.
2. Attach the rubber band to the clip of the board.
3. Placing it on a flat surface, try to move the board by pulling at the rubber band. Note the stretch in the band.
4. Now put the board with the book on the 4 pencils.
5. Again pull it. You will find that the board moves easily. Note the stretch in the band. Is it more or less than before?

The pencils in this case act like wheels and reduce friction, thus making movement easier.

Pulleys

Pulleys are used to lift heavy loads.

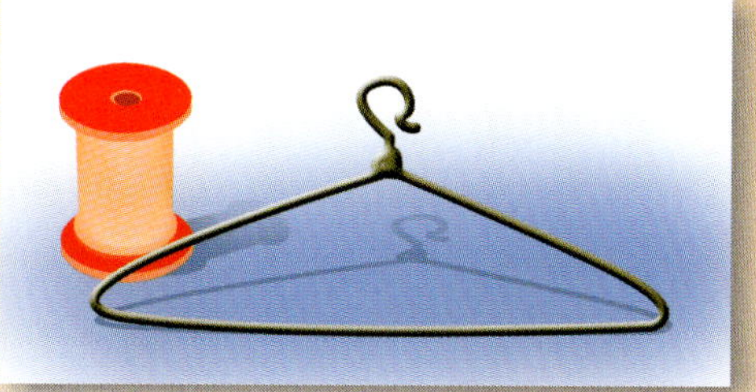

Make your own pulley

1. Take a wire coat hanger and break the horizontal rod.
2. Bend it to the shape shown.
3. Pass both the straight ends through an empty cotton reel. The reel should turn freely.
4. Bend the ends down to prevent the wire from spreading.

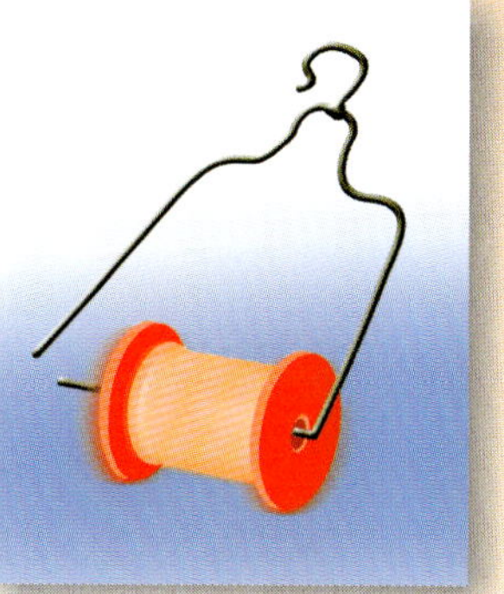

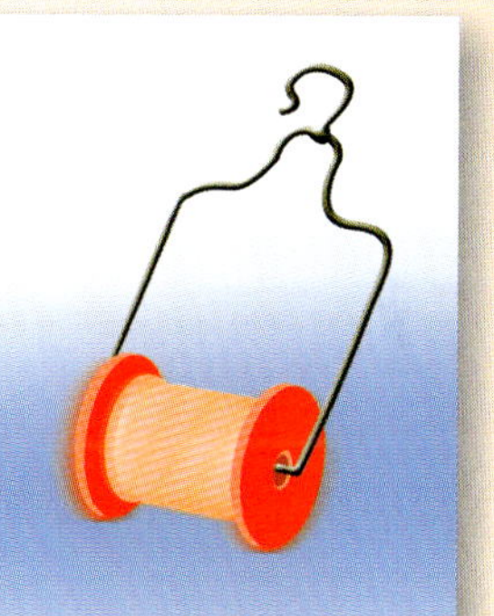

Let's experiment with pulleys

1. Put two chairs back-to-back about 3 feet apart.
2. Tie a stick across the top of the chairs.
3. Attach a cord to the centre of the stick. Thread it through a pulley.
4. Tie a load to the pulley. The load should be kept on the ground.
5. Now pull the free end of the cord and see how the pulley lifts the load.
6. Pass the cord through another pulley closer to the stick, and tie it to the stick.
7. Pull again.

   Do you think it is easier to lift the weight with two pulleys? If not, what advantage does the second pulley provide?

   Note that you can now pull downwards.

Check your strength

Take two rods, tie a strong rope to one of the rods, and wrap it around both of them. Then ask two friends to hold the two rods and pull them apart while you pull the free end of the rope. See who wins.

Isn't this a good trick? But, can you explain how it works? No matter how hard your friends try, they will never be able to pull the rods apart.

This is because the rods and the rope act like a pulley system, and help you overcome their big pull with your little effort.

Gears

Gears are machines that transfer force from one point to another by toothed wheels. Gears in a car carry forces from the engine to the wheels.

Gears can operate in two ways. They can make large forces from small ones and small forces from large ones.

Make your own gears

1. Collect some bottle caps.
2. Straighten the edges of the caps and make them as flat as possible.
3. With a nail and a hammer, make holes in the exact centres of the caps.
4. Place two caps on a board so that the teeth-like projections mesh together.
5. Fix them in place with board pins. Make sure that the caps turn freely.
6. Turn one of the caps. In which direction does the second cap move?
7. Try with three caps.